Contents

D0971046

Copyright..2

Disclaimer 3

About the Author 4

Bonus Content..5

What is Cross Training 6

Benefits of Cross Training 8

Interpreting Cross Training Hybrid Workouts 11

Acronyms 13

Cross Training Base Exercises 18

Hybrid Beginner Workouts 26

Benchmark Workouts................................28

Bodyweight WODs 46

Regular WODs 50

Running WODs 72

Endurance WODs 76

No-Nonsense Nutrition 80

Supplementation......................................90

Conclusion..97

Copyright

Cross Training 101: Build the Ultimate Athletic Physique

Third Edition – March 2014.
Written by Scott James

A Shredded-Society Publication
www.Shredded-Society.com
Copyright © 2014
All rights reserved.

Disclaimer

The information provided in this book is designed to provide helpful information on the subjects discussed. This book is not meant to be used, nor should it be used, to diagnose or treat any medical condition. For diagnosis or treatment of any medical problem, consult your own physician. The publisher and author are not responsible for any specific health or allergy needs that may require medical supervision and are not liable for any damages or negative consequences from any treatment, action, application or preparation, to any person reading or following the information in this book. References are provided for informational purposes only and do not constitute endorsement of any websites or other sources. Readers should be aware that the websites listed in this book may change.

I recommend consulting a doctor to assess and/or identify any health related issues prior to making any dramatic changes to your diet or exercise regime.

About the Author

Scott James has been addicted to all things fitness, health and nutrition for nearly a decade.

With a large amount of hype surrounding the fitness industry, as well as the dieting and supplementation niches Scott thought it was the right time to come forward and debunk the myths and scams within the industry.

All information conveyed in Scott's books is tried and tested - no false hope or bad information is shared.

Scott believes that when an individual is equipped with the correct knowledge and a plan of action that he will provide in his books they are unstoppable.

Scott is not here to make money, he's here to make a different and guide you on your journey to unlocking the new, better you.

Bonus Content

As a token of our appreciation Shredded-Society would like to give you access to our Cross Training 101 exclusive bonus content.

<u>You're only a click away from receiving:</u>

The 5 most effective Cross Training workouts

A guide detailing the only Cross Training equipment you should use while training

Exclusive pre-release access to our latest eBooks

Free Shredded Society eBooks during promotional periods

Simply go to:
www.Shredded-Society.com/Crosstraining101.html
to receive this bonus content from Shredded-Society

As this is a limited time offer it would be a shame to miss out, I recommend grabbing these bonuses before reading on.

What is Cross Training

Cross Training is a functional style of athletic training that focuses on improving the cardiovascular fitness as well as muscular endurance of all individuals in a hardcore, yet fun filled and encouraging manner.

Instead of having a prescribed workout that is followed day in, day out dedicated Cross Trainers often participate in different workouts on a daily basis in order to shock the body, ensuring it is able to adapt to any situation... as that truly is the real definition of fitness (as opposed to how many times you can bench press 225lbs).

Runners improve their respiratory system and cardiovascular endurance; weightlifters improve their strength and power.

<u>Wouldn't it be great to target all aspects of your fitness via one hybrid style of training?</u>

By combining elements of both conventional cardiovascular aerobic style exercises, heavy compound anaerobic exercises and lighter endurance focused anaerobic and bodyweight exercises this is possible.

By following this style of routine you will notice improvements in all areas of your fitness including increased respiratory system and cardiovascular endurance, increased stamina, increased power & strength, coordination and balance will greatly improve, flexibility, mobility and range of motion will improve along with agility and speed thanks to bursts of high intensity interval training.

The end goal of this intensive style of training is to equip an individual with a body that is capable of performing any and every physically demanding task presented to them, whether this be lift heavy objects off the ground, project their bodyweight through the air or run 3 miles – you'll be ready.

If you're ready to start a cross training style workout regime it's time to say goodbye to the treadmills and lateral pull-down machines at your local gym. Instead, you will start utilising Olympic barbells, sandbags, kettlebells, rowers, ropes and rings amongst other functional equipment.

I will go further in to depth regarding these workouts later in the book.

Benefits of Cross Training

If a regular workout is a light cup of coffee that slowly wakes you up, Cross Training is like a double shot of caffeine straight to the brain.

As mentioned above if you're looking to build an unbreakable physique than this is the style of training for you! Now, let's look at some of the other associated benefits - these include:

Intensity

These hybrid style workouts are fast paced and intense (as the emphasis is on speed and total weight being lifted), they are generally much shorter than a regular weight lifting workout – however since the workout is condensed it is constant non-stop movement, there is no time to stop and talk to your gym partner between sets like you normally would as you are constantly working against the clock to better yourself, time trials are half of the fun.

Creates Athletes

All exercises performed are high power functional movements, this is highly emphasised. Unlike bodybuilding you will not waste time on low power isolation movements. The major benefit here is now that the focus has been taken off vanity and looks it has been put on pure performance – the core strength, stamina, coordination, agility and balance you will develop will transfer over to sports and all other facets of life.

Time

The number one excuse for individuals not following a workout regime is the constraint of time; yes its true – working out takes time.
However, workouts are short – you will find the majority of workouts in this book range from 15 to 20 minutes each in duration. Therefore they are fast and more effective than a regular workout in which you spend an hour on a cross trainer mindlessly staring at the wall.

Measureable Results

These workouts provide you with measureable and repeatable data; this can be used to verify that your fitness level is increasing. With a series of 'bench mark' workouts you can easily assess your progress, which in turn keeps the fire alive to keep you pushing towards your goals.

Life Changing

Change your body, change your life, and change your world...
Cross Training workouts build mental strength, grit and
confidence; a tough workout will emotionally push you
beyond your limits. When you ignore the voice inside your
head that says 'it's too hard' or 'I can't do that last rep' and
push past it unbreakable confidence is built – then anything
is possible.

Community

Aspects of health and fitness, specifically the training portion
encourage community, both in the gym and online.
People encourage and support each other through out their
workouts – you will never have to work out alone again
unless you want to, as the bond formed between training
partners make training truly fun. It is very rarely you will
find an individual that is as passionate about a particular
pastime as yourself however this could not be further from
the truth when it comes to working out we are all teammates
that push and pray for each other.

Interpreting Cross Training Hybrid Workouts

Unlike a normal workout regime, in which you determine in advance the exercises and sets you are going to be doing in advance this hybrid form of training takes an entirely different approach and uses the 'WOD' system, which is an acronym for **W**orkout **o**f the **D**ay. Various gyms and websites throughout the world issue their own WOD on a daily basis.

The majority of athletes follow a 3/1 training schedule.
This means you will partake in 3 consecutive workout days, followed by 1 rest day.
This however, is only a recommendation – many advanced athletes choose to do 5/2 and a variety of other schedules to suit their end state goals and recovery time.

Now let's take a look at a WOD and analyse it.

This WOD was taken directly from P Selter's 'WOD Bible'

TUES 131126

Six rounds for time of:
Run 500 meters
185 pound Deadlift, 21 reps

Analysis:

Tuesday 131126 – this workout was published on Tuesday, the 26th of November 2013.

Six rounds for time of: Run 500 meters, 185 pound deadlift for 21 reps – this WOD consists of 2 exercises, a 500 meter run and a 185lb deadlift, you are to complete 5 rounds of these exercises in the fastest time possible (use a timer to record so you can compare your score to others). The complete workout would look like this:

Warm up (don't forget to stretch and warm up before beginning, it is crucial to avoid injury)

Start timer

500 meter run

185lb deadlift for 21 reps

500 meter run

185lb deadlift for 21 reps

500 meter run

185lb deadlift for 21 reps

500 meter run

185lb deadlift for 21 reps

500 meter run

185lb deadlift for 21 reps

500 meter run

185lb deadlift for 21 reps

Stop timer

Acronyms

Before we get into the WODs themselves it is imperative you familiarise yourself with the following acronyms in order to read the workout of the day correctly (or use this page as a reference guide when reading the workout if necessary).

1RM: Your 1RM is your max lift for one rep

AHAP: as heavy as possible

AMRAP: As many rounds as possible

ATG: Ass to Grass

BP: Bench press

Box: Another term used for gym

BS: Back squat

BW: Body weight

Chipper: A WOD containing many different exercises and reps

CLN: Clean

C&J: Clean and jerk

C2: Concept II rowing machine

DL: Deadlift

DOMS: Delayed onset muscle soreness

DU: Double under

EMOM: Every minute on the minute

For Time: Timed workout, perform as quickly as possible and record score.

FS: Front squat

GHR(D): Glute ham raise (developer). Posterior chain exercise, similar to a back extension. Also, the device that allows for the proper performance of a Glute Ham Raise.

GHR(D) Situp: Situp performed on the GHR(D) bench.

GPP: General physical preparedness, another word for fitness

GTG: Grease the Groove, a protocol of doing many sub-maximal sets of an exercise throughout the day

H2H: Hand to hand; refers to Jeff Martone's kettlebell "juggling" techniques

HSPU: Hand stand push up. Kick up into a handstand (use wall for balance, if needed) bend arms until nose touches floor and push back up.

HSQ: Hang squat (clean or snatch). Start with bar "at the hang," about knee height. Initiate pull. As the bar rises drop into a full squat and catch the bar in the racked position. From there, rise to a standing position

IF: Intermittent Fasting

KB: Kettlebell

KBS: Kettlebell swing

KTE: Knees to elbows.

MEBB: Maximum Effort Black box, term coined by Mike Rutherford.

MetCon: Metabolic Conditioning workout

MP: Military press

MU: Muscle ups. Hanging from rings you do a combination pull-up and dip so you end in an upright support.

OH: Overhead

OHS: Overhead squat. Full-depth squat performed while arms are locked out in a wide grip press position above (and usually behind) the head.

PC: Power clean

Pd: Pood, weight measure for kettlebells

PR: Personal record

PP: Push press

PSN: Power snatch

PU: Pull-ups or push ups depending on the context in WOD

Rep: Repetition. One performance of an exercise.

RM: Repetition maximum.

ROM: Range of motion.

Rx'd: As prescribed, without any adjustments.

SDHP: Sumo deadlift high pull

Set: A number of repetitions. e.g., 34sets of 8 reps, often seen as 4x8, means you do 8 reps, rest, repeat, rest, repeat, rest, repeat.

SPP: Specific physical preparedness, aka skill training.

SN: Snatch

SQ: Squat

SS: Starting Strength; Mark Rippetoe's great book on strength training basics

Subbed: Substituted

T2B: Toes to bar. Hang from bar. Bending only at waist raise your toes to touch the bar, slowly lower them and repeat.

Tabata: A form of interval training comprised of 20 seconds on, 10 seconds off repeated for 8 rounds.

TGU: Turkish get-up

The Girls: A series of benchmark workouts named after girls

The Heroes: Brutal benchmark workouts in honour of fallen soldiers

TnG: Touch and go, no pausing between reps

WO: Workout

WOD: Workout of the day

WU: Warm up

YBF: You'll Be Fine

Cross Training Base Exercises

Clean

A weight lift starting from the ground that requires using the upwards momentum of a deadlift, jump, and front squat to bring the weight up to the shoulders. Most commonly done with a barbell.

Kettlebell clean

A clean using a kettlebell.

Hang clean

A clean starting from the hanging position (standing upright, holding the barbell with straight arms &legs), instead of starting from the ground.

Power clean

a clean without dropping into a full front squat to catch the weight. A minimal jump and dip of the body separates a power clean from a regular clean.

Clean and jerk

a full clean, then jerk the barbell overhead after arriving at the shoulders.

Triceps dip

Support yourself on shoulder-width handholds (usually

parallel bars) with straight arms, bend the elbows to a 90-degree angle, and then straighten arms.

Ring dip

a triceps dip on gymnastics rings.

Jerk

a lift starting from the shoulders & ending overhead, using the upward momentum of a hip thrust.

Push jerk

Lifting the weight overhead in combination with two small dips in the knees to drive the weight upwards.

Split clean and jerk

a combination of the clean and the jerk, ending with a split foothold position.

Muscle up

A combination of a pull up to dip, which allows you to lift yourself up and over a handhold from a hanging position.

Bar muscle up

a muscle up using a pull-up bar.

Ring muscle up

a muscle up using the gymnastics rings.

Pull up

Starting from a hanging position, using your upper body strength to pull your chin up and over your handhold.

Front lever pull up

a pull up while holding your body in a horizontal line.

Jumping pull up

Quick, small pull ups in which your feet return back to the ground after each jump.

Kipping pull up

a pull up using added momentum from a "kip", which uses extension & flexion of the body to provide a "swing".

Weighted pull up

a pull up with a weight around your waist.

Push press

pushing a weight from the shoulders to overhead in combination with a small dip in the knees.

Shoulder press

pushing a weight from the shoulders to overhead, with no movement (no knee-dip) in the lower body.

Kettlebell press

a shoulder press using a kettlebell, done one arm at a time.

Push-ups

From a plank position, lowering yourself to the ground and back up using your arms.

Modified push up

a push up with your knees on the ground, or with your hands on a raised surface (incline push up)

Handstand Push Up

From a handstand, bending your arms to lower your head to the ground, then back up.

Squat

most commonly meaning a back squat, with a barbell resting on the shoulders, bending at the knees and sinking into a sitting position, then straightening back up.

Air squat

a full squat with no extra weight (barbell or dumbbells).

Overhead squat

a squat while holding a weight overhead.

Front squat

a squat with the barbell racked in the front, at shoulder level.

Jumping squats

jumping upwards after rising from each squat.

Pistol

a one-legged squat that requires immense strength and balance.

Snatch

A lift that brings the weight from the ground up overhead while dropping into an overhead squat position, then rising out of the squat. Most commonly done with a barbell.

Dumbbell snatch

a snatch done with a pair of dumbbells.

Kettlebell snatch

a snatch done with a kettlebell.

Hang snatch

a snatch with the weight starting from a hang.

Ball slams

lifting a weighted ball overhead, slamming it down, and picking it up immediately from the rebound.

Bench press

from a laying position on a bench, using your arms to raise and lower a barbell from the chest.

Box jump
Jump up and back down from a box (usually 20-24 inches high).

Burpee
Starting from a standing position, descend into a plank, do a chest-to-ground push up, then jump back up as high as you can & repeat.

Dumbbell split lift
pushing a pair of dumbbells overhead in combination with a jump into a split foothold.

Deadlift
a barbell lift starting from the ground, in which one engages the legs and core to lift the weight from the ground to a hang.

Double under
 Two turns of the skipping rope per jump.

Farmer's Walk
Grab two heavy plates or dumbbells (one in each hand) and walk as far as you can without dropping them.

Handstand Push Ups
Push-ups are pretty standard, but a handstand push up is

extremely difficult. You must be able to push-press your own bodyweight before you can do a handstand push up. Click the link for handstand help.

Knees to elbows

using your abdominal muscles to bring your knees to your elbows while in a hanging position.

Kettlebell swing

swinging a Kettlebell through the range of motion from a hang to overhead.

Rope Climb

Climb up a rope. It's helpful to learn the different foot-wraps for rope climbing, click on the link for instructions & tips.

Thruster

a barbell lift starting from shoulder height, in which one performs a front squat, then pushes the barbell overhead during the rise to standing position.

Toes to Bar

using your abdominal muscles to bring your toes to the bar from which you are hanging by your hands.

Wall ball shot

with a weighted ball, descend into a squat, and heave the ball upwards at the wall during the upwards movement of the squat, then catch the ball on the rebound.

V-Up

From a lying position, use your abs to bring your arms and legs up to meet in the middle.

Hybrid Beginner Workouts

The following workouts are fantastic for beginners, they are tough and will test you but do not contain advanced exercises like muscle ups etc. I recommend starting with these workouts as an introduction.

Beginner Workout 1
3 rounds for time:
10 burpees
20 squats
30 situps

Beginner Workout 2
8 intervals – 20 seconds work – 10 seconds rest:
Pushups
Situps
Squats

Beginner Workout 3
5 rounds for time:
10 tuck jumps
15 back extensions

Beginner Workout 4
2 rounds for time:
400m run
50 lunges (25 per leg)

Beginner Workout 5
For time:
100 pushups
50 situps

Beginner Workout 6
3 rounds for time:
20 burpees
30 squats
40 situps

Beginner Workout 7
4 rounds for time:
15 tuck jumps
25 situps

Beginner Workout 8
For time:
100 burpees

Beginner Workout 9
5 rounds for time:
20 burpees
10 situps
20 squats

Beginner Workout 10
For time:
5km run

Benchmark Workouts

The Girls

These benchmark workouts are designed to measure the improvements in your performance, they are to be performed irregularly (they can take the place of your regular WOD on occasion).

Angie
For time (complete all reps of each exercise before moving on)
100 pull-ups
100 push-ups
100 sit-ups
100 squats

Barbara
5 rounds for time
20 pull-ups
30 push-ups
40 sit-ups
50 squats

Chelsea
Each minute on the minute for 30 minutes of:
5 pull-ups
10 push-ups
15 squats

Cindy
As many rounds as possible in 20 minutes of:
5 pull-ups
10 push-ups
15 squats

Diane
21-15-9 reps, for time

Deadlift 225lbs
Handstand push-ups

Elizabeth
21-15-9 reps, for time
Clean 135lbs
Ring Dips

Fran
21-15-9 reps, for time
Thruster 95lbs
Pull-ups

Grace
30 reps for time
Clean and jerk 135lbs

Helen
3 rounds for time
400 meter run
1.5 pood kettlebell swing x 21
Pull-ups 12 reps

Isabel
30 reps for time
Snatch 135 pounds

Jackie
For time
1000 meter row
Thruster 45lbs – 50 reps
Pull-ups – 30 reps

Karen
For time
Wall-ball – 150 shots

Linda (aka '3 bars of death')
10/9/8/7/6/5/4/3/2/1 rep rounds for time
Deadlift 1.5 BW
Bench 1x BW
Clean ¾ BW

Mary
As many rounds as possible in 20 minutes of:
5 handstand push-ups
10 1 legged squats
15 pull-ups

Nancy
5 rounds for time
400 meter run
overhead squat 95lbs x 15

Annie
50-40-30-20-10 rep rounds for time
Reps of:
Doubleunders
Sit-ups

Eva
5 rounds for time
Run 800 meters
2 pood KB swing, 30 reps
30 pull-ups

Kelly
Five rounds for time
Run 400 meters
30 box jump, 24 inch box
30 wall ball shots, 20 pound ball

Lynne
5 rounds for max reps (not timed)
Bodyweight bench press (if you weight 170lbs, you will bench

170lbs)
Pull-ups

Nicole
As many rounds as possible in 20 minutes of:
Run 400m
Max rep pull-ups

The Heroes

The Hero workouts are workouts created in honour of brave athletic soldiers and law enforcement officers who have fallen while serving for their country. These workouts are not for the faint hearted – they are extremely tough, not designed for beginners. The Heroes, just like The Girls are to be used irregularly for assessing your progress instead of performing the regular WOD.

JT
21-15-9 reps, for time
Handstand push-ups
Ring dips
Push-ups

Michael
3 rounds for time
Run 800 meters
50 back extensions
50 Sit-ups

Murph
For time, partition the pull-ups, push-ups and squats as necessary
1 mile run
100 pull-ups
200 push-ups
300 squats
1 mile run

Daniel
For time

50 pull-ups
400 meter run
95 pound thruster – 21 reps
800 meter run
95 pound thruster – 21 reps
400 meter run
50 pull-ups

Josh
For time
95 pound overhead squat – 21 reps
42 pull-ups
95 pound overhead squat – 15 reps
30 pull-ups
95 pound overhead squats – 9 reps
18 pull-ups

Jason
For time
100 squats
5 muscle-ups
75 squats
10 muscle-ups
50 squats
15 muscle-ups
15 squats
20 muscle-ups

Badger
3 rounds for time
95 pound squat clean – 30 reps
30 pull-ups
Run 800 meters

Joshie
3 rounds for time
40 pound dumbbell snatch – 21 reps right arm
40 pound dumbbell snatch – 21 reps left arm
21 L pull-ups
Note: snatches are full squat snatches

Nate
As many rounds as possible in 20 minutes
2 muscle-ups
4 handstand push-ups
8 2-pood kettlebell swings

Randy
For time
75lb power snatch – 75 reps

Tommy V
For time
115lb thruster – 21 reps
15ft rope climb – 12 ascents
115lb thruster – 15 reps

15ft rope climb – 12 ascents
115lb thruster – 9 reps
15ft rope climb – 6 ascents

Griff
For time
Run 800 meters
Run 400 meters backwards
Run 800 meters
Run 400 meters backwards

Ryan
For time
five rounds of:
7 muscle-ups
21 burpees
Note: each burpee terminates with a jump one foot above
max standing reach

Erin
For time
five rounds of:
40lb dumbbell split clean – 15 reps
21 pull-ups

Mr Joshua
For time
five rounds of:
Run 400 meters
30 glute-ham sit-ups
250lb deadlift – 15 reps

DT
For time
five rounds of:
155lb deadlift – 12 reps
155lb hang power clean – 9 reps
155lb pound push jerk – 6 reps

Danny
Maximum number of rounds in 20 minutes of:
24 inch box jump – 30 reps
115lb push press – 20 reps
30 pull-ups

Hansen
For time
five rounds of:
30 reps – 2 pood kettlebell swing
30 burpees
30 glute-ham sit-ups

Tyler
For time
five rounds of:
7 muscle-ups
95lb Sumo-deadlift high-pulls – 21 reps

Lumberjack 20
For time
20 deadlifts (275lbs)
Run 400m
20 KB swings (2 pood)
Run 400m
20 overhead squats (115lbs)
Run 400m
20 Burpees
Run 400m
20 Pull-ups (Chest to Bar)
Run 400m
20 Box jumps (24″)
Run 400m
20 DB Squat Cleans (45lbs each)
Run 400m

Stephen

For time

30-25-15-10-5 rep rounds of:

GHD sit-up

Back extension

Knees to elbow

95lb stiff legged deadlift

Garrett
For time
3 rounds of:
75 squats
25 ring handstand push-ups
25 L-pull-ups

War Frank
For time
3 rounds of:
25 muscle-ups
100 squats
35 GHD sit-ups

McGhee
Rounds in 30 minutes
275lb deadlift – 5 reps
13 push-ups
9 box jumps 24 inch box

Paul
For time
5 rounds of:
50 double unders
35 knees to elbows
185lb overhead walk – 20 yards

Jerry
For time
Run 1 mike
Row 2k
Run 1 mile

Nutts
For time
10 handstand push-ups
250lb deadlift – 15 reps
24 box jumps – 30 inch box
50 pull-ups
100 wallball shots – 20lbs, 10"
200 double-unders
Run 400 meters with a 45lb plate

Arnie
For time
with a single 2 pood kettlebell:
21 Turkish get-ups – right arm
50 swings
21 overhead squats – left arm
50 swings
21 overhead squats – right arm
50 swings
21 Turkish get-ups – left arm

The Seven
For time
Seven rounds of:
7 handstand push-ups
135lb thruster – 7 reps
7 knees to elbows
245lb deadlift – 7 reps

7 burpees
7 Kettlebell swings – 2 pood
7 pull-ups

RJ
For time
five rounds of:
Run 800 meters
15ft rope climb – 5 ascents
50 push-ups

Luce
For time
wearing a 20lb vest, perform 3 rounds of:
run 1K
10 muscle-ups
100 squats

Johnson
Rounds in 20 minutes
245lb deadlift – 9 reps
8 muscle-ups
155lb squat clean – 9 reps

Roy
For time
five rounds of:
225lb deadlift – 15 reps
20 box jumps – 24 inch box
25 pull-ups

Adam Brown
For time
two rounds of:

295lb deadlift – 24 reps
24 box jumps – 24 inch box
24 wallball shots – 20lb ball
195lb bench press – 24 reps
24 box jumps – 24 inch box
24 wallball shots – 20lb ball
145lb clean – 24 reps

Coe
For time
ten rounds of:
95lb thruster – 10 reps
10 ring push-ups

Severin
For time
50 strict pull-ups
100 push-ups release hands from floor at the bottom
Run 5k
Note: wear 20lb weighted vest if possible

Helton
For time
3 rounds of:
Run 800 meters
50lb dumbbell squat cleans - 30 reps
30 burpees

Jack
Max rounds in 20 minutes
115lb push press – 10 reps
1.5 pood KB swings – 10 swings
10 box jumps 24 inch box

Forrest

For time
3 rounds of:
20 L-pull-ups
30 toes to bar
40 burpees
800 meter run

Bulger

For time
Ten rounds of:
Run 150 meters
chest to bar pull-ups – 7 reps
135lb front squat – 7 reps
Handstand push-ups – 7 reps

Brenton

For time
Five rounds of:
Bear crawl 100 feet
Standing broad-jump – 100 feet
Note: wear 20lb weighted vest if possible

Blake

For time
4 rounds of:
100 foot walking lunge with 45lb plate held overhead
30 box jumps – 24 inch box
20 wallball shots – 20lb ball
10 handstand push-ups

Colin

For time
6 rounds of:

Carry 50lb sandbag 400 meters
115lb push press – 12 reps
12 box jumps – 24 inch box
95lb sumo deadlift high-pull – 12 reps

Thompson
For time
10 rounds of:
15ft rope climb – 1 ascent
95lb back squat – 29 reps
135lb barbells farmer carry – 10 meters
Note: begin the rope climbs seated on the floor

Whitten
For time
5 rounds of:
22 kettlebell swings – 2 pood
22 box jumps – 24 inch box
run 400 meters
22 burpees
22 wall ball shots – 20lb ball

Bull
For time
2 rounds of:
200 double-unders
135lb overhead squat -50 reps
50 pull-ups
run 1 mile

Rankel
AMRAP – 20 minutes
225lb deadlift – 6 reps
burpee pull-ups – 7 reps

2 pood KB swings – 10 swings
run 200 meters

Holbrook
Each round for time
Ten rounds of:
115lb thruster – 5 reps
10 pull-ups
100 meter sprint
1 minute rest

Ledesma
AMRAP – 20 minutes
5 parallette handstand push-ups
10 toes through rings
20 pound medicine ball cleans – 15 reps

Wittman
For time
7 rounds of:
1.5 pood KB swings – 15 swings
95lb power clean – 15 reps
15 box jumps – 24 inch box

Mccluskey
For time
3 rounds of:
9 muscle-ups
15 burpee pull-ups
21 pull-ups
run 800 meters

Weaver
For time

4 rounds of:
10 L-pull-ups
15 push-ups
15 chest to bar pull-ups
15 push-ups
20 pull-ups
15 push-ups

Abbate
For time
Run 1 mile
155lb clean and jerk – 21 reps
run 800 meters
155lb clean and jerk – 21 reps
Run 1 mile

Hammer
Each round for time
135lb power clean – 5 reps
135lb front squat – 10 reps
135lb jerk – 5 reps
20 pull-ups
Note: rest for 90 seconds between rounds

Moore
Rounds in 20 minutes
15ft rope climb – 1 ascent
run 400 meters
max rep handstand push-ups

Wilmot
For time
6 rounds of:

50 squats
25 ring dips

Moon

For time
7 rounds of:
40lb dumbbell hang split snatch – 10 reps right arm
15ft rope climb – 1 ascent
40lb dumbbell hang split snatch – 10 reps left arm
15ft rope climb – 1 ascent
Note: alternate feet in the split snatch sets

Small

For time
3 rounds of:
row 1000 meters
50 burpees
50 box jumps – 24 inch box
run 800 meters

Bodyweight WODs

All of the following WODs are based entirely upon body weight exercises such as push-ups, pull-ups, burpees and dips – these WODs are ideal for days that you are unable to make it to your gym, or if you are travelling. With hybrid based Cross training workouts there are literally no excuses not to get your workout in, for these all you need is 20~ minutes of spare time and an open space.

Death by pull-ups
With a continuously running clock do one pull-up
The first minute, 2 pull-ups the second minute, 3 pull-ups the third minute... continuing as long as you are able.
Use as many sets each minute as needed.

WOD
30 muscleups

WOD
120 pull-ups and 120 dips

GI Jane
100 burpee-pull-ups

WOD
As many rounds as possible in 20 minutes of:
15 pull-ups
30 push-ups
45 squats
Walking lunge 400m

Tabata Something Else
Complete 32 intervals of 20 seconds of work followed by 10 seconds of rest where

the first 8 intervals are pull-ups, the second 8 are push-ups, the third 8 intervals
are sit-ups, and finally, the last 8 intervals are squats. There is no rest between
exercises.

WOD
50-40-30-20-10
reps of:
pull-ups
ring dips

WOD
150 burpees

WOD
handstand push-ups: 15-13-11-9-7-5-3-1
Lpullups:
13-5-7-9-11-13-15

WOD
3 rounds of:
Run 800m
50 pull-ups

WOD
50 burpees
jump 12" above max reach each one.

WOD
sit-ups
50 doubleunders
50 sit-ups
50 walking lunges
50 sit-ups
50 burpees
50 sit-ups

WOD
7 rounds of:
10 One legged squats, alternating
12 ring dips
15 pull-ups
10 rounds of:
12 burpees
12 pull-ups

WOD
4 rounds of:
Run 400m
50 squats

WOD
5 rounds of:
15 L-pull-ups
30 push-ups
45 sit-ups

WOD
5 rounds of:
25 inverted burpees
25 pull-ups
25 burpees
(Inverted burpee: Starting supine, kip (or situp
and roll) to standing, kickup
to handstand)

WOD
30 handstand push-ups
10 pull-ups
20 handstand push-ups
20 pull-ups
10 handstand push-ups
30 pull-ups

WOD
50-30-20
reps of:
doubleunders
push-ups
pull-ups

WOD
Run 800 meters
40 L pull-ups
Run 800 meters
40 strict pull-ups
Run 800 meters
40 kipping pull-ups

WOD
5 rounds of:
50 squats
30 pull-ups
15 handstand push-ups

WOD
50 ring dips
Run 400 meters
50 push-ups
Run 400 meters
50 handstand push-ups
Run 400 meters

WOD
3 rounds of:
50 doubleunders
75 squats

WOD
5 rounds of:
50 squats
100 rope jumps

Regular WODs

WOD
With a continuously running clock do one muscleup
the first minute, 2 muscleups
the second minute, 3 muscleups
the third minute, as long as you can. Run 400m.
Repeat ladder for deadhang pull-ups. Run 400m. Repeat
ladder for kipping pull-ups.

WOD
3 rounds of:
50 push-ups
50 sit-ups
50 squats

WOD
100 squats
100 pull-ups
200 push-ups
300 squats
100 lunges

Bodyweight Fran
21-15-9 reps of:
pull-ups
burpees

Segmented Bodyweight Fran
21-15-9
reps of:
pull-ups
push-ups
squat jumps to 12" above max reach

WOD
50-35-20 reps 3 rounds of:

handstand push-ups
pull-ups

WOD
Repeat for 15 minutes:
20 seconds of pull-ups
20 seconds of sit-ups
20 seconds of squats

WOD
100 pull-ups
200 push-ups
300 squats
50 sit-ups

WOD
As many rounds as possible in 20 minutes of:
25 pull-ups
50 push-ups
75 squats

WOD
As many rounds as possible in 20 minutes of:
25 handstand push-ups
50 One legged squats, alternating
75 pull-ups

WOD
As many rounds as possible in 20 minutes of:
10 L pull-ups
20 squats
M/
ME

WOD
100-75-50-25 reps:
sit-ups
flutterkicks (4 count)

Leg levers

The Reckoning
Run 1 mile
100 bodyblasters (burpee-pull-ups-kneestoelbows)
Run 1 mile

WOD
Cummulative Lhold
for total of 5:00. Use bar, rings, or floor.
Stop timer when you drop out of position. Record total time
it takes to get 5:00.

WOD
100 sit-ups
100 flutterkicks (4 count)
100 leg levers

WOD
With a continuously running clock do one Handstand
pushup the first minute, 2
pull-ups the second minute, 3 handstand push-ups the third
minute and 4 pull-ups the
4th minute continuing in this pattern as long as you are able.
If your pace falls
behind the count, continue to alternate exercises while
recording reps for a total
of twenty minutes.

WOD
handstand push-ups 5x5
Maximize range of motion by using blocks or chairs.

Running Tabata Something Else
Tabata pull-ups, 1 round
Run 1 mile
Tabata push-ups, 1 round
Run 1 mile

Welcome to Chick-fil-A
Denham Springs FSU (# 03319)
Denham Springs, LA
Operator: Jeffrey Hollifield
225-791-4411

CUSTOMER COPY
3/2/2017 9:00:27 AM
DRIVE THRU

2 CEC Bagel   6.90
    + No Cdmt

Sub. Total: 6.90
Tax: $0.72
Total: $7.62

Change $0.00
Discover: $7.62

Register:2   Tran Seq No: 1451408
Cashier:Andrea
It was a pleasure serving you!
Have a wonderful day.

Discover
Card Num : XXXXXXXXXXXXX9859
Terminal : KA220866651002
Approval : 00237R
Sequence : 005733

Tabata sit-ups, 1 round
Run 1 mile
Tabata squats, 1 round
Run 1 mile

WOD
For best time.
10-20-30 reps of:
squat
handstand push-ups
squat
pull-ups

Running with Angie
100 pull-ups
Run 1 mile
100 push-ups
Run 1 mile
100 sit-ups
Run 1 mile
100 squats
Run 1 mile

Murph Tribute
Run 1 mile
50 pull-ups
100 push-ups
150 sit-ups
200 squats
Run 1 mile
50 pull-ups
100 push-ups
150 sit-ups
200 squats
Run 1 mile

WOD
50 ring dips

100 squats
50 ring dips
100 squats
50 ring dips
WOD
21-15-9 reps of:
handstand push-ups
Inverted pull-ups

WOD
5 rounds of:
50 walking lunges
15 handstand push-ups

Deck of Cards
Take a deck of cards, shuffle. Face cards are 10, Aces are 11, numbered cards as
valued. Flip each card and perform the movement and the number of reps specified.
Cycle whole deck.
Hearts push-ups
Diamonds pull-ups
Spades sit-ups
Clubs squats
Jokers Run
1 mile

Deck of Cards (Core Variation)
Take a deck of cards, shuffle. Face cards are 10, Aces are 11, numbered cards as
valued. Flip each card and perform the movement and the number of reps specified.
Cycle whole deck.
Hearts burpees
Diamonds mountain
climbers (4ct)
Spades flutterkicks
(4ct)

Clubs sit-ups
Jokers Run
400m

WOD

21-15-9 reps of:
ring push-ups
ring dips

WOD

5 rounds of:
30 handstand push-ups
30 pull-ups

WOD

5 rounds of:
Max ring dips in 1:00
Rest 1:00
Max ring push-ups in 1:00
Rest 1:00

WOD

100 squats
20 handstand push-ups
30 pull-ups

WOD

100 squats
9 handstand push-ups
200 squats
15 handstand push-ups
100 squats
21 handstand push-ups

WOD

7 rounds of:
Max rep dips
Max rep pull-ups

Rest as needed.

WOD
100 Lpullups
ME/C
100 squats
40 pull-ups
80 squats
32 pull-ups
60 squats
24 pull-ups
40 squats
16 pull-ups
20 squats
8 pull-ups

WOD
80 squats
10 handstand push-ups
60 squats
20 handstand push-ups
40 squats
30 handstand push-ups
20 squats

WOD
10 rounds of:
10 pull-ups
20 push-ups
30 squats

WOD
4 rounds of:
50 squats
5 muscleups

WOD
As many rounds as possible in 20 minutes of:
7 handstand push-ups
12 Lpullups

WOD
50 squats
50 pull-ups
50 walking lunges
50 kneestoelbows
5 handstand push-ups
50 sit-ups
5 handstand push-ups
50 squats
50 pull-ups

WOD
100 squats
30 muscleups
100 squats
M/S
4 rounds of:
25 lunges
50 squats

WOD
100 squats
25 sit-ups
100 squats
25 sit-ups
100 squats
25 kneestoelbows
100 squats
25 handstand push-ups

WOD
3 rounds of:
100 squats

50 ring dips
30 Lpullups

WOD
5 rounds of:
5 handstand push-ups
5 muscleups

WOD
2 rounds of:
35 squats
35 kneestoelbows
35 squats
35 sit-ups
35 lunges
35 squats

WOD
21-18-15-12-9-6-3 reps of:
squats
Lpullups
kneestoelbows

WOD
7 rounds of:
35 squats
25 push-ups
15 pull-ups

WOD
5 rounds of:
10 dips
15 pull-ups
20 handstand push-ups

WOD
5 rounds of:
100 squats
20 lunges
35 push-ups

WOD
21-15-9 reps of:
Body blasters (burpeepullupkneestoelbows)
box jump burpees
Belushi burpees (on jump turn 180 degrees)
Burpee Jacks (plank jack to jumping jack)
WOD
Give 30 minutes to handstand and hand walking practice.

WOD
3 rounds of:
100 squats
25 Lpullups
30 handstand push-ups

WOD
3 rounds of:
7 muscleups
100 squats

WOD
5 rounds of:
50 squats
30 handstand push-ups

WOD
3 rounds of:
100 squats
20 ring push-ups
12 pull-ups

WOD
5 rounds of:
50 squats
15 ring push-ups

WOD
3 rounds with 2:00 rests between each round:
50 squats
30 pull-ups
40 push-ups
50 squats

WOD
10-9-8-7-6-5-4-3-2-1
pull-ups
ring push-ups
handstand push-ups

WOD
5 rounds of:
9 handstand push-ups
9 pull-ups

WOD
2 rounds of:
21 lunges
21 pull-ups
21 squats
21 ring dips
21 handstand push-ups

WOD
As many rounds as possible in 20 minutes:
10 False grip ring pull-ups (rings to chest)
10 ring dips (go as deep as possible)

WOD
5 rounds of:
50 squats
21 ring dips
21 handstand push-ups

WOD
21 pull-ups
50 squats
21 kneestoelbows
18 pull-ups
50 squats
18 kneestoelbows
15 pull-ups
50 squats
15 kneestoelbows
12 pull-ups
50 squats
12 kneestoelbows

WOD
7 rounds of:
20 ring dips
20 pull-ups
20 lunges

WOD
25 squats
25 sit-ups
25 lunges
25 handstand push-ups
25 push-ups
25 kneestoelbows
25 dips
25 pull-ups

WOD
As many rounds as possible in 20 minutes of:
10 pull-ups
10 ring dips
10 walking lunges

Bad Snake
100 rope jumps
21 kneestoelbows
50 Push ups
15 LPullups
100 rope jumps
15 kneestoelbows
35 Push ups
12 LPullups
100 rope jumps
12 kneestoelbows
20 Push ups
9 LPullups

Seppuku
10 rounds of:
10 Lpullups
10 ring push-ups
10 kneestoelbows

20 pieces of Angie
20 rounds of:
5 pull-ups
5 push-ups
5 sit-ups
5 squats

Burning Rings of Fire
10 ring push-ups
10 Archer push-ups (5 each side)
10 ring Flyes
10 Wide Grip ring push-ups

10 Single leg ring push-ups (5 each leg)
10 Pseudoplanche ring push-ups
10 Jackknife ring push-ups
10 Dive Bomber ring push-ups
10 Elevated ring push-ups
10 ring push-ups

WOD
25 handstand push-ups
25 squats
25 pull-ups
25 One legged squats
25 muscleups

WOD
3 rounds of:
100 squats
50 ring dips

WOD
100 squats
21 handstand push-ups
30 pull-ups
100 squats
30 pull-ups
21 handstand push-ups
100 squats

WOD
5 rounds of:
20 squats
20 push-ups
20 pull-ups

WOD
50-40-30-20-10 reps
pull-ups
squat jumps

WOD
50 burpees
75 flutterkicks (4count)
100 push-ups
150 sit-ups

WOD
Run 1 mile
30 pull-ups (chest to bar)
60 push-ups

WOD
2 rounds:
Max push-ups 2:00
Max sit-ups 2:00
Max flutterkicks 2:00
Max squats 2:00

WOD
100 squats
20 handstand push-ups
30 pull-ups
100 squats
30 pull-ups
20 handstand push-ups
100 squats

WOD
15 rounds for max reps:
pull-ups, 30 seconds on / 30 seconds off

WOD
Run 10 minutes max effort
200 squats
Run 10 minutes max effort

WOD
50 squats
50 jumping pull-ups
50 steps walking lunge
50 kneestoelbows
50 handstand push-ups
50 sit-ups
50 dips
50 squats
50 push-ups

WOD
Run 1 mile
21 Lpullups
Run 1 mile
21 bar muscleups
Run 1 mile
21 ring muscleups

WOD
4 rounds of:
50 walking lunges
50 squats
Run 400m

WOD
4 rounds of:
5 muscleups
50 straightleg
lifts on rings

WOD
5 rounds of:
10 burpees
20 box/bench jumps
30 push-ups
40 squats
50 lunges
pistols (1 leggedsquats)

3x10 on each leg
Hold a rock or other heavy object to increase the load.

WOD
Practice your kipup
for 20 minutes, with hands or without.
Kipup consists of lying flat supinated to explosively standing up.

Playing with push-ups
Run 100m
20 push-ups
5 burpees
15 clap push-ups
5 burpees
10 chestslap
push-ups
5 burpees
5 fingertip push-ups
Run 100m
15 push-ups
5 burpees
10 clap push-ups
5 burpees
10 chestslap
push-ups
5 burpees
5 fingertip push-ups
Run 100m
10 push-ups
5 burpees
10 clap push-ups
5 burpees
10 chestslap
push-ups
5 burpees
5 fingertip push-ups

Balboa
4 rounds of:
100 jump ropes
Run 400 meters
10 Bodyblasters (burpeepullupkneestoelbows)

Crouching Tiger
50 squats
25 push-ups
50 pistols
25 fingertip push-ups
50 side lunges
25 knuckle push-ups
50 walking lunges
25 diamond push-ups

Fractured Runny Angie
Run 400 meters
25 pull-ups
25 push-ups
25 sit-ups
25 squats

WOD
Run 5k, but every 5:00 do 50 push-ups and 50 squats.

WOD
20-16-12-8-4 reps of:
Onearm push-ups
Onelegged squats

WOD
50 flutterkicks
50 sit-ups
Run 400m
100 flutterkicks
100 sit-ups
Run 400m

WOD
4 rounds of:
50 push-ups
50 sit-ups
50 4ct flutterkicks

WOD
250 squats
20 muscleups
250 squats

WOD
1 round Tabata sprints
1 round Tabata squats, rest position is in the squat
There is no rest between exercises.

WOD
150 squats
50 push-ups
21 pull-ups
Run 800 meters
21 pull-ups
50 push-ups
150 squats

WOD
50 Lpullups
50 handstand push-ups
50 pistols
50 kneestoelbows

WOD
As many rounds as possible in 12 minutes of:
10 push-ups
15 sit-ups
20m walking lunge

WOD
Spend a cummulative total of 5 minutes in a hand stand, or head stand.

WOD
21-15-9 reps of:
lunges (Each leg ½ rep)
sit-ups
burpees

WOD
5 rounds of:
50 mountain climbers (4 count)
25 sit-ups

WOD
5 rounds of:
100 jumping jacks
100 mountain climbers

Prison Workout
Burpees 20-19-18-17-16-15-14-13-12-11-10-9-8-7-6-5-4-3-2-1
walk 25m after each set

Ash
3 rounds, 90 seconds per station of:
burpees
push-ups
box/bench jumps
pull-ups
Double Unders
squats

WOD
Run 1 mile
60 push ups
40 dips

20 handstand push-ups
10 pistols (each leg ½ rep)
20 handstand push-ups
40 dips
60 push ups
Run 1 mile

WOD
3 rounds of:
Run 800m
30 burpees
30 kneestoelbows

WOD
4:00 of sit-ups
2:00 of push-ups
2:00 of flutterkicks
1:00 of deadhang pull-ups

Ivan the Terrible
90 seconds of jumping rope
50 lunges
50 push-ups
50 sit-ups
90 seconds of jumping rope
40 lunges
40 push-ups
40 sit-ups
90 seconds of jumping rope
30 lunges
30 push-ups
30 sit-ups
90 seconds of jumping rope
20 lunges
20 push-ups
20 sit-ups
90 seconds of jumping rope
10 lunges

10 push-ups
10 sit-ups

Long Cycle Burpees
50 rounds of:
1 squat
1 pushup
1 situp
1 superman
1 tuck jump

WOD
5 rounds of:
30 second isometric squat hold
20 squats
30 seconds isometric leaning rest
20 push-ups

WOD
50 jumping jacks
50 push-ups
50 tuck jumps
50 sit-ups
50 mountian climbers(50 each leg)
50 squats
50 jumping jacks

WOD
10 rounds of:
30 seconds handstand
30 seconds isometric squat

Running WODs

The following WODs are all based around running, no equipment besides a track/oval are necessary. Maximum effort is to be used unless otherwise stated.

WOD
2 mile run for best time

WOD
Max distance in 30 minutes

WOD
1 round Tabata uphill sprints (20:10 x 8)

WOD
4 rounds of:
5:00 max distance
3:00 recovery

WOD
3 rounds:
5km run with 30 second recovery between rounds

WOD
1.2km uphill sprint
Rest 1:00
1.2km downhill jog
Rest 1:00
Repeat

WOD
1:00 sprint, 1:00 rest
1:00 sprint, 0:50 rest
1:00 sprint, 0:40 rest
1:00 sprint, 0:30 rest

1:00 sprint, 0:20 rest
1:00 sprint, 0:10 rest
1:00 sprint, 0:20 rest
1:00 sprint, 0:30 rest
1:00 sprint, 0:40 rest
1:00 sprint, 0:50 rest
1:00 sprint, 1:00 rest

WOD
10x100m with 2:00 rest
8x200m with 2:00 rest
4x400m with 5:00 rest
8 rounds of:
80 second sprint, 40 second rest

WOD
3 rounds of:
1:00 sprint, 1:00 recovery
2:00 sprint, 2:00 recovery
3:00 sprint, 3:00 recovery

WOD
3:00 sprint, 3:00 recovery
2:00 sprint, 2:00 recovery
1:00 sprint, 1:00 recovery
2:00 sprint, 2:00 recovery
3:00 sprint, 3:00 recovery

WOD
4x800m with 2:00 rest
Run 10k. Run second half faster than the first.

WOD
3 rounds of:
100m sprint, Rest same amount of time you finished the sprint

200m sprint, Rest same amount of time you finished the sprint
300m sprint, Rest same amount of time you finished the sprint

WOD
3 rounds of:
200m sprint, Rest same amount of time you finished the sprint
400m sprint, Rest same amount of time you finished the sprint
600m sprint, Rest same amount of time you finished the sprint

WOD
10 rounds of:
1:00 sprint, 1:00 recovery

WOD
8 rounds of:
10 seconds sprint, 5 seconds recovery

WOD
0:45 sprint, 0:45 recovery
1:30 sprint, 1:30 recovery
3:00 sprint, 3:00 recovery
6:00 sprint, 6:00 recovery
3:00 sprint, 3:00 recovery
1:30 sprint, 1:30 recovery
0:45 sprint, 0:45 recovery

WOD
16 rounds of:
10 seconds sprint, 20 seconds recovery

WOD
4x200m + 4x400m + 2x1000m

Rest 1:00, 1:30, and 2:00 per interval distance, respectively.

WOD
200m sprint, Rest same amount of time you finished the sprint
400m sprint, Rest same amount of time you finished the sprint
600m sprint, Rest same amount of time you finished the sprint
400m sprint, Rest same amount of time you finished the sprint
200m sprint, Rest same amount of time you finished the sprint

WOD
1 mile time trial
Rest 60 seconds
2x400m sprint
Rest 60 seconds between sprints

WOD
4x200m
2x400m
Rest 60 seconds between sprints

Endurance WODs

The following WODs were created for those who are looking for an extended gruelling workout. Several of these workouts will take hours to complete, I would not recommend these to beginners.

Speed Demon
For time:
Run 3km
Row 3k
Run 1km

Burpee Mile
For time:
Cover a 1600m distance by performing burpees.
Perform a large jump with each rep.

Triple Murph
3 rounds:
1 mile run
100 pullups,
200 pushups,
300 squats
1 mile run
First round to be completed with a weighted vest, partition as necessary
Second round is to be completed without partitions
Third round to be partitioned as necessary

The 500 Challenge
500 pullups
500 pushups
500 situps
500 flutterkicks

500 squats
Partition as necessary

1,500 Rep WOD
10 rounds of:
100 jump ropes
10 burpees
10 situps
10 pushups
10 squats
10 pullups

The Longest Mile
400m of burpees
400m walking lunges
400m bear crawl
400m reverse straight-legged bear crawl

Painstorm XXIV
Run 100m
50 burpees
Run 200m
100 pushups
Run 300m
150 walking lunges
Run 400m
200 squats
Run 300m
150 walking lunges
Run 200m
100 pushups
Run 100m
50 burpees

Frenzy
10 rounds of:
Max burpees 60 seconds

Max pullups 60 seconds
Max tuck jumps 60 seconds
Max jumping jacks 60 seconds
Max distance running 60 seconds

Station 4:00
Station A: running
Station B: burpees
Station C: pullups
Station D: squat jumps
Station E: bear crawl or lunges
Round 1: 5:00 at each station, for total of 25:00.
Round 2: 12:00 at each station, for total of 1:00:00.
Round 3: 30:00 at each station, for total of 2:30:00.
Round 4: 1:00 at each station, for total of 5:00.

Filthy Fifteen Miles
60 rounds of:
Run 400m
3 handstand pushups
2 pistols
1 muscle up

October Breeze
110 minutes: March with rucksack.
15 minutes: Eat, hydrate, stretch, change clothes if necessary.
60 minutes: Run at half marathon pace.
60 minutes: Complete 1000 walking lunges.
30 minutes: 5 rounds: ring dips 1:00, rest 1:00, ring pushups 1:00, rest 1:00
60 minutes: Run at half marathon pace.
15 minutes: Eat, hydrate, stretch, change clothes if necessary.
30 minutes: Complete Angie, max intensity.
15 minutes: Sprint 10x100m with 1:00 rests.
15 minutes: Complete 100 burpees.
30 minutes: 4 rounds: 50 squats, 5 muscle ups. Sub 3/3 for MU if necessary.
30 minutes: 500 situps.

10 minutes: Run 1 mile.

Long ladder of doom
Begin with 2 muscle ups, then 4 pistol squats + 2 muscleups,
then 6 one-armed pushups + 4 pistol squats + 4 muscle ups,
continuing to the rest of the workout at 30.
2 muscle-up
4 pistols
6 one-armed pushups
8 L-pullups
10 toes to bar
12 skin the cats
14 ring dips
16 5 foot broad jumps
18 pushups
20 air squats
22 box jumps
24 lunges
26 double unders
28 burpees
30 jingle-jangles

A Frogman's Christmas
100 dead hang pull-ups
250 push-ups
500 sit-ups
Run 3 miles

No-Nonsense Nutrition

'Eat Like a Predator, Not Like Prey'

In order to build lean muscle, recover and have sufficient energy levels it is crucial that your diet is in check. The Paleo diet is the diet of choice amongst fitness enthusiasts.

What is the Paleo diet you may ask? The Paleo diet (short for Paleolithic) aka. The Caveman diet is comprised solely of unprocessed foods, essentially the Paleo diet advocates eating foods that existed prior to the advent of modern farming.

Grains, dairy, alcohol and sugar and are all a no go.

Should you choose to follow the Paleo diet, which is a more of a lifestyle change than a diet, your diet will be based on:

Garden vegetables
Lean meats
Nuts
Seeds

These foods encourage a high protein, low carbohydrate and moderate to high healthy fat intake. Calories are not counted strictly, as Paleo is more nutritional content focused, I do however suggest slightly restricting your caloric intake. Paleo will allow you to restrict your caloric intake while still providing ample nutrients and sufficient energy for rigorous activity.

When shopping for the above foods in the supermarket you will notice that they are all around the perimeter of the supermarket, this is commonly where all the perishable foods are located, meanwhile all the processed foods containing preservatives and long shelf lives are located within the aisles of the supermarket.

Simple carbohydrates should be avoided at all costs, as they are known for being the major cause of health issues. Simple carbohydrates, unlike complex carbohydrates will not provide you with any sustainable energy to perform rigorous activity.

The Paleo diet has many long term health benefits including:

Detoxification of the Body
You are no longer consuming processed foods and are, therefore, eliminating a whole range of bad substances from your body, such as hidden sugars, sodium, additives, coloring, and artificial flavors.

Quality of Nutrients

You will be consuming a much larger amount of nutrients than before – vegetables, healthy fats, nuts, seeds, berries and fruit are all LOADED with vitamins and minerals. With the elimination of grains, your body will now also be able to absorb these nutrients far more efficiently.

Body Re-composition

The majority of individuals that partake in the Paleo diet experience sustained fat loss and an increase in lean muscle mass.

No More Bloating & Gas

A large amount of fiber is consumed when following the Paleo diet (vegetables are high in fiber). A diet rich in fiber, combined with sufficient water intake and minimal sodium, decreases the bloating that is common when on a western diet.

Feel Fuller for Longer

Unlike other diets that deprive you of calories, the Paleo diet will keep you feeling full – the meats included in the diet are high in protein, with the vegetables and fruits containing just the right amount of carbohydrates while still providing a large amount of fiber to keep you feeling fuller for longer.

Less Allergies

When following the Paleo diet, the amount of foods consumed that are known to contain allergens is drastically reduced.

Reduction in Inflammation

Scientific research indicates that inflammation may very well be a leading factor behind cardiovascular disease. Risk while following the Paleo diet is minimized – many of the foods included in the diet are anti-inflammatory (due to a large portion of foods containing high content of Omega 3 fatty acids).

More Energy!

By eating healthy whole foods, you will no longer rely on strong coffees riddled with sugar or energy drinks for energy. You will feel more alert and will no longer require these beverages –they will eventually lead to type 2 diabetes and insulin resistance if consumed excessively.

Increased Insulin Sensitivity

After consuming foods high in simple sugars for a long period of time, your body desensitizes itself to these simple sugars. Eventually your body will begin to reject these simple sugars as a source of energy –instead it will begin to store the sugars as fat.

The Paleo diet does not contain any foods high in simple sugars (with the exception of fruit, however, this is fructose and is recommended to only be consumed infrequently in small portions).

Improved Digestion with Better Gut Flora

Processed foods containing large amounts of sugars and man-made fats are known to cause inflammation within the intestinal tract. Eating these bad foods for a prolonged period of time can lead to leaky gut syndrome (the correct medical term for this condition is Hyperpermeable Intestines). Leaky gut syndrome is when the intestinal lining becomes porous with large holes developing in the lining; the result of this is large undigested food molecules, yeast, toxins and waste flowing freely into your bloodstream.

Improvement in Sleep Quality

Many individuals that partake in the Paleo diet report an increase in quality of sleep. Due to an increase in energy on the Paleo diet, reliance on caffeine is no longer required. Caffeine is well known for causing a plethora of sleeping issues.

Reduction in Risk of Diseases

The Paleo diet's main focus is to avoid all of the foods that are known to harm your health. You will not find any unhealthy foods on the Paleo approved foods list. By only eating the whole foods that are approved on the Paleo diet (the foods that cavemen ate), you will be limiting your risk of disease simply but not consuming foods that we know are linked to them.

Like all diets, the Paleo diet does have several disadvantages the major disadvantages being the minimal variety in terms of meals and recipes. Social outings can also be quite hard when following a Paleo based diet – although salads are always a viable option.

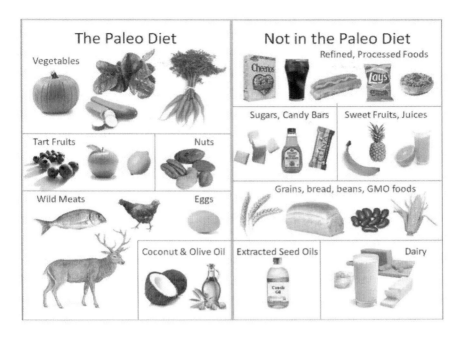

The above diagram portrays an outline of the foods included and excluded in the Paleo diet

Your diet doesn't have to be boring and bland just because processed and sweet foods are a no-go. On the following pages you will find several of my all-time favourite Paleo dishes, they're easy to prepare, nutritious and most importantly of all delicious!

Sweet Potato and Spinach Omelette

Ingredients:

2 cups sweet potato, diced
1 onion, diced
2 tbsp. olive oil
3 cups baby spinach
5 eggs
Salt and pepper

Method:

Pre-heat oven to 390F.
In an oven proof dish, place sweet potato, diced onion, olive oil, salt and pepper. Bake in oven for 25 minutes, or until sweet potato is cooked.
Place a pan on high heat with water and bring to the boil.
Add spinach and cook for 1-2 minutes until soft.
Drain well, removing excess water.
Spread sweet potato mixture along base of an oven proof dish.
Layer with spinach and pour over beaten eggs.
Bake in oven for 15-20 minutes or until eggs are cooked.
Remove from oven and leave to cool for 5 minutes before serving.

Coconut Chicken Curry

Ingredients:

2 chicken breasts, sliced
2 tbsp. olive oil
1 onion, diced
2 garlic cloves, finely chopped
2 tbsp. red curry paste
1 tsp. turmeric, ground
400ml coconut milk
12 bay leaves

Method:

Heat 1 tbsp. of olive oil in a wok or fry pan, add chicken and cook until golden brown.
Remove from pan.
Place remaining oil into the pan and fry onion and garlic until slightly browned, add red curry paste and turmeric and stir for 1 minute.
Add coconut milk and bay leaves and leave to simmer on low heat for 15 minutes.
Cool slightly before serving.

Blueberry Sorbet

Ingredients
2 cups blueberries
½ banana
1/3 cup coconut milk
1½ tbsp. honey
1 egg white

Instructions
Using an electric blender, blend together blueberries, banana, coconut milk and honey until well combined.
Fold blueberry mixture into the beaten egg white.
Pour into an ice-cream container and freeze overnight.
To serve, cut into slices.

Supplementation

Fitness supplements are a multi-billion dollar industry – but do all the supplements on the market do what they claim? Certainly not. No powder will 'Increase your squat by 128% as proven by college studies' or give you the 'ripped abs you deserve, in 3 weeks or less.' If it sounds too good to be true, it probably is. Supplements serve the purpose they suggest: they simply 'supplement' your diet. Providing you are hitting your caloric intake and macronutrients each day, supplementation may contribute up to 5%.

As long as newcomers continue to get conned into purchasing all of these magical powders and pills, the supplementation industry will continue to thrive. Did you know that many supplements don't even undergo any testing or approval before they are allowed to be sold on the shelves?

The supplements listed below are the supplements I have been personally using for years and would recommend. These are the basics, and they have been proven true, unlike many of the other supplements full of fluff and filler ingredients that are on the market.

Protein

The primary purpose of protein powder is to assist you in reaching your macronutrient breakdown, and, depending on your daily intake, it can be hard (and time consuming) to get your protein intake for the day in via solid food – this is where protein powder comes in to play. 1 scoop of protein powder has between 25 and 30 grams of protein.

Protein is protein. It doesn't vary as much between brands as the manufacturers will lead you to believe. No protein is twice as effective as another, and there is no such thing as a male and female specific protein so why should you pay twice as much? Keep it simple and get the right type of protein as opposed to focusing on the brand.

WPI (Whey Protein Isolate)
Whey Protein Isolate is a fast acting type of protein. It begins working almost immediately and is best suited to a post-workout meal. It has no other place in your diet.

WPC (Whey Protein Concentrate)
This is a much cheaper version of WPI, and acts over a much longer period of time. This can be used at any time, but still doesn't compare to, for example, egg protein, as far as effectiveness. WPC is a lot cheaper than WPI and is almost as good; it really provides value for the money.

Casein Protein (Slow Release)
This is a slow acting protein, and generally lasts about 5 hours in your system. This is ideal before bed, or for a midnight snack. If you have the budget, I'd purchase some of this just to take before bed as it will fuel your body for quite some time.

Multivitamin

Multivitamins can greatly help your diet. They're ideal for helping to supplement the vitamins and minerals that your body is deficient in. When putting together a diet, we quite often limit how much variety we have. This will lead to us neglecting vital vitamins. The best way to take care of this is simply taking a decent multivitamin. Most of them on the market are fairly priced and provide you with everything you will need from vitamin B to Zinc.

Fish Oil

Fish oil contains EFA (essential fatty acids). It is available in both capsule and liquid form and has many benefits, including a healthier blood cholesterol profile and improved bone health – no more squeaky joints! It also assists in protecting against major diseases, such as cancer. Fish oil also assists in increasing the serotonin levels within your body which results in an overall increase in happiness and well-being. Recent studies also show that fish oil may have an influence on muscle protein synthesis.

When selecting fish oil, ensure it is high in EPA/DHA as these are the main omega 3 fatty acids.

I recommend consuming between 2 – 3G per day (capsules generally come in 1000mg and 1500mg).

Vitamin C

No other vitamin has as many positive effects on the body as vitamin C. As vitamin C is not stored in your body, it needs to be replenished daily. Without supplementation, reaching your daily vitamin C intake can be quite difficult.

Vitamin C is required for the growth and repair of tissues in all parts of your body. It is used to form collagen, a protein used to make skin, scar tissue, tendons, ligaments, and blood vessels. It is also essential for the healing of wounds, and for the repair and maintenance of your cartilage, bones, and teeth. Vitamin C also helps with blood pressure by strengthening the walls of your arteries. It can also prevent damage to cells caused by aging as well as help reduce levels of stress.

For athletes, vitamin C will keep testosterone levels high by supporting a lower ratio of cortisol to testosterone. This will help your body keep up that top level of performance you require on a daily basis.

I recommend consuming 1g of vitamin C per day. As vitamin C is water soluble, any excess amount of this vitamin will simply be urinated out within 24 hours.

Caffeine/Coffee

Caffeine is an alkaloid compound found in the seeds, leaves and fruits of various plants. Caffeine is a mild stimulant and drug that acts upon the brain and central nervous system. According to The New York Times, caffeine is known as "the most popular drug used in sports today." Caffeine is apparent in coffee, tea, and pre-workout supplements and capsules to name a few variations.

Caffeine has been involved with many studies over the years, reinforcing its positive effects in fat loss, mental focus and overall physical performance.

The greatest benefit of having caffeine before your workout is its fat burning properties. High amounts of caffeine in black coffee will increase your metabolism, which makes you burn more calories throughout the day. Having coffee before exercise enhances that effect. Also, caffeine and other compounds found in coffee act as an appetite suppressant, making you consume less overall.

Several studies have demonstrated a link between caffeine intake before exercise and increased athletic performance. A report published in *Sports Medicine* refers to caffeine as a "powerful ergogenic aid," and mentions that athletes can "train at a greater power output and train longer" after caffeine consumption. Another study published in the *British Journal of Sports Science* found that subjects who consumed coffee before running 1500 meters on the treadmill completed their run 4.2 seconds faster than the control group, on average. To gain an extra edge in your training sessions, coffee might be just what you need.

Along with increased energy to push through tough workouts, caffeine provides an increase in mental focus as well. Improved focus will help keep workouts productive and effective.

Researchers at the University of Illinois found that subjects who consumed caffeine prior to exercise experienced less muscle pain during their workout than their non-caffeinated counterparts. What conclusion can we draw from this? You can complete more reps at a higher resistance during your weight training sessions, and run faster and longer during your cardio workouts with the assistance of caffeine.

Consuming caffeine in the form of coffee helps protect your body from diseases. Coffee contains large amounts of antioxidants, which protect against damage from free radicals. According to a 2011 study published in *Critical Reviews in Food Science and Nutrition*, coffee consumption has an inverse correlation with diabetes, Parkinson's disease, Alzheimer's disease, and certain forms of cancer.

I recommend consuming 200 – 300mg of caffeine before your workouts (in the form of black coffee), however, individuals have different stimulant tolerances. I would experiment with various doses, but do not exceed this amount. It is beneficial to 'cycle' caffeine as the human body quickly builds a tolerance to the stimulant properties of caffeine and will, therefore, not be as effective. A 1:1 on:off ratio works well.

Conclusion

As you can now see the Cross Training hybrid style of workout has spread through the fitness community like wildfire, and with good reason too. Individuals of all ages can partake in a community based, fun and competitive workout regime that is constantly changing, you will force your body to adapt to any challenge you are faced with and is ideal for not only building lean muscle and explosive power – but also an unbreakable mindset to match.

No longer do you need to spend countless hours on the treadmill staring at a wall; no longer do you need to perform the same monotonous workout routine week after week.

Join the revolution today!

I hope you enjoyed reading this book as much as I enjoyed writing it.